Stonehenge

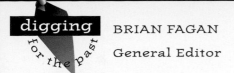

BRIAN FAGAN

General Editor

Stonehenge

Caroline Malone
and Nancy Stone Bernard

OXFORD

UNIVERSITY PRESS

To Aaron, Colin, and Catie

OXFORD
UNIVERSITY PRESS

Oxford   New York
Auckland Bangkok Buenos Aires Cape Town Chennai
Dar es Salaam Delhi Hong Kong Istanbul Karachi Kolkata
Kuala Lumpur Madrid Melbourne Mexico City Mumbai Nairobi
São Paulo Shanghai Singapore Taipei Tokyo Toronto
and an associated company in
Berlin

Design: Kingsley Parker
Layout: Lenny Levitsky
Picture research: Fran Antmann

Library of Congress Cataloging-in-Publication Data

Bernard, Nancy S. (Nancy Stone)
Stonehenge / Nancy S. Bernard and Caroline Malone.
p. cm. — (Digging for the past)
Includes bibliographical references and index.
Summary: Examines the site of the huge stone monument known as
Stonehenge, discussing who built it, as well as theories on when, how,
and why it was constructed.
ISBN 0-19-514314-0 (alk. paper)
1. Stonehenge (England)—Juvenile literature. 2. Wiltshire
(England)—Antiquities—Juvenile literature. 3. Megalithic
monuments—England—Wiltshire—Juvenile literature. [1. Stonehenge
(England) 2. Megalithic monuments. 3. England—Antiquities.] I. Malone,
Caroline. II. Title. III. Series.
DA142 .B47 2002
936.2'319—dc21
                                          2001007113

9 8 7 6 5 4 3 2 1

Printed in Hong Kong on acid-free paper

Contents

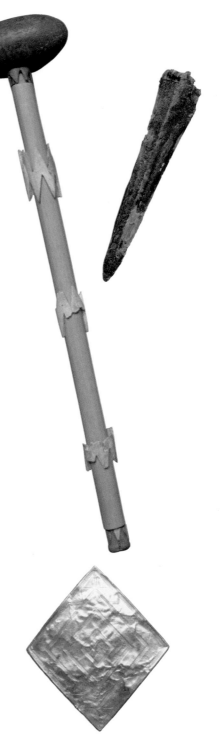

Where and When

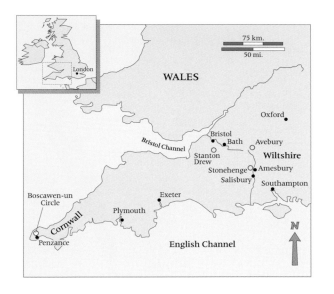

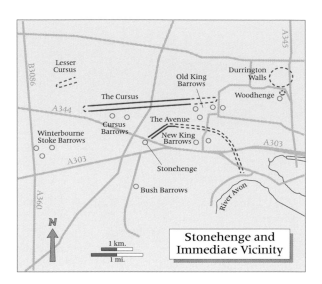

Stonehenge and Immediate Vicinity

Archaeological History

1802 ▶
William Cunnington and Sir Richard Colt Hoare open more than 600 barrows in Wiltshire, including 200 near Stonehenge

1919–26 ▶
Restorations made for safety of the visiting public; excavator Colonel William Hawley investigates nearly half of the monument

1958–59 ▶
Using a 60-ton mobile crane, archaeologists lift a few stones, encase them in felt-padded steel cages, and reset them

1966 ▶
Three large pits are found dating to as early as 8000 B.C.

1979 ▶
Atkinson and J. G. Evans reopen a 1954 trench and uncover a human burial from the Beaker period with the flint arrowheads that had killed the man in his backbone

◀ **1901**
Professor William Gowland supervises the erection of a fallen Sarsen and works to ensure the safety of visitors

◀ **1950**
Professors R. J. C. Atkinson, Stuart Piggott, and J. F. S. Stone agree to excavate and produce a definitive report

◀ **1963**
A Sarsen falls without warning; it is reset and several others are put in concrete, leaving only seven upright Sarsens in their original sockets

◀ **1979**
Discovery of a hole for another stone next to the Heel Stone

Ancient History

8000–3100 B.C.	◄ Three holes dug that could have held pine posts to support a wooden structure
2950–2900 B.C.	◄ Construction of a henge, a circular ditch and bank, 490 feet in diameter with a single entrance; inside the ditch 56 pits dug, later known as the Aubrey Holes
2900–2550 B.C.	◄ Stonehenge abandoned
2550–2400 B.C.	◄ New activity at Stonehenge with several wooden buildings constructed
2550–1600 B.C.	◄ Main period of Stonehenge building; in as many as six stages, stones were brought to the site, taken down, and then rebuilt into new patterns
1500 B.C.	◄ Stonehenge abandoned, never to be used again by its builders

Introduction

The greatest rock group of Britain? It's not a band. It's Stonehenge. From a distance, these rocks don't look like a big deal. They look like a bunch of rocks plopped down on a slight hill on Salisbury Plain, in a part of England called Wessex, about 80 miles west of London. But as you get closer, the standing stones loom bigger and bigger until finally, when you walk nearer they tower over you.

Still standing are five great stones capped by three massive lintels, the crosspieces on top of the stones, and seventeen uprights with lintels. Six of the smaller Bluestones are all that are left of possibly forty. It is a wreck of a stone building that once included about 162 stones. But even in this ruined state, today the stones are recognized as a monumental complex, an important symbol of prehistory in Europe that has been designated a World Heritage Site by the United Nations Educational, Scientific, and Cultural Organization (UNESCO).

Lots of questions might occur to you as you look at these stones. What are they? Who built them, and why did they do it? When did modern people first notice them? Where did the stones come from, and how did they get there? Why do some people connect them with an ancient people called the Druids? Was it constructed all at once, or were different parts built at different times? Are there similar sites elsewhere in the British Isles? Why was it abandoned? What is its future?

These are questions that have puzzled visitors to Stonehenge, historians, and archaeologists for hundreds of years. We're going to try to answer these questions now.

1

Imaginary Tales and Early Depictions

The first known writings about Stonehenge appeared in the 12th century, in histories of Britain written by Henry of Huntingdon and Geoffrey of Monmouth. Neither of these men knew why it was there, but Geoffrey, at any rate, thought if you don't know something, it's better to make up a story. So he modified the legend that King Arthur and his magician, Merlin, brought the great stones across the sea from Ireland. This was one of the earliest among many imaginary and misleading tales created to explain the origins of Stonehenge.

This illustration from a 14th-century manuscript— depicting the magician Merlin building Stonehenge—is a very rare early drawing of the monument.

Geoffrey guessed that Merlin's magical creation took place in about the fifth century A.D. But he was not even close. Today, we know that what eventually became a stone circle began to be built around 3000 B.C.—some 5,000 years ago—and continued to be remodeled for another 1,500 years. The actual meaning of the name Stonehenge is "hanging stones," because people thought the stones were hanging from the uprights.

In the 16th century, a teacher and antiquarian named William Camden wrote accounts of ancient places that were tremendously popular. His book *Britannia*, which covered centuries of British history, was so influential that it was printed again and again for 250 years after it was first published around 1586. The book's popularity was not diminished by some of Camden's far-fetched ideas. For instance, he thought that giants had built stone circles like Stonehenge. He also described the monument as "a mad construction" in the edition of *Britannia* published in 1600. By 1695, an imaginative but quite inaccurate illustration was included.

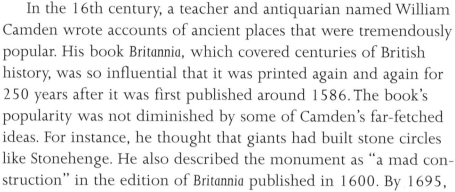

This engraving of Stonehenge was made for William Camden's book Britannia *in 1695. The artist had probably never seen the monument, because he placed it in a mountainous landscape, depicted the stones incorrectly, and surrounded it with a wall.*

During the reign of England's King James I, in the early 17th century, the king commissioned the great architect Inigo Jones to make a survey of the site. What resulted—published in 1652, after Jones's death, by his assistant James Webb—with very geometric and architectural drawings, was the first book entirely about Stonehenge. But Jones could not believe that the ancient Britons could have built such a "beautiful, elegant" monument and wrongly concluded that Stonehenge was built by the Romans.

Later in the 17th century, John Aubrey was one of the first serious scholars of ancient sites in Britain. He

was especially fascinated with stone circles and standing stones. In *Monumenta Britannica*, which he wrote in about 1665, Aubrey recognized that these places had existed long before the Romans occupied Britain in the first century B.C. Aubrey also cautiously suggested that Druids, an ancient Celtic people, may have used these places as temples.

Aubrey, a careful and accurate observer, noticed 56 holes just inside the bank and ditch surrounding Stonehenge, which in the early 20th century were named the Aubrey Holes in his honor. Copies of the manuscript of *Monumenta Britannica* were circulated and the original was deposited in Oxford University's Bodleian Library, but the work was not published until 1982, 285 years after Aubrey died.

For the most part, however, Stonehenge was mistakenly thought to be the site of hidden treasure during this period. Many fortune hunters dug up the land around Stonehenge in the 17th and 18th centuries, recklessly tossing aside dirt and rocks in their eager quest for wealth. No one found any riches, but unfortunately much of the center was disturbed as a result of all this treasure hunting. Ironically, modern archaeologists have found a treasure trove—of information, not gold or jewels—in what was carelessly excavated.

About 1721, the Reverend Thomas Hayward, who owned the land where Stonehenge is found, let loose a colony of rabbits around the monument. They burrowed beneath much of the ground, destroying further what could have been evidence for how and when different parts of Stonehenge were built.

In the 18th century, Dr. William Stukeley, first a physician and later a clergyman, made the next useful observations about Stonehenge and other ancient sites. He traveled extensively around

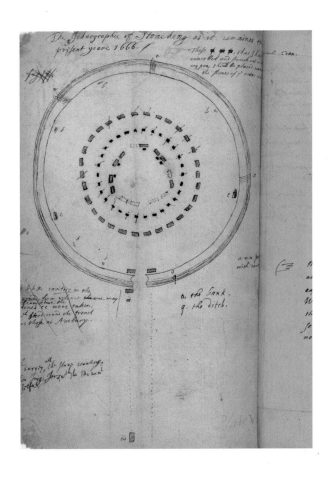

John Aubrey made this sketch of Stonehenge in 1666. The dotted lines at the bottom indicate the Avenue. He noted five extra "cavities in the ground" just inside the ditch and bank, which were later named the Aubrey Holes in honor of this unusually careful observer.

Britain, making accurate drawings and writing descriptions of hundreds of prehistoric monuments, which he later published. He is known as the "father of field archaeology," but he drew many of his ideas, especially the Druid association, from John Aubrey's *Monumenta Britannica*, which he copied from the original manuscript kept in Oxford University's Bodleian Library. Beginning in 1721 and continuing through the summer of 1724, he concentrated on Stonehenge.

The suggestion that the Druids were associated with Stonehenge persists even today. A few people still think of Stonehenge as a Druid monument, even though archaeologists debunked the Druid myth years ago. We now know that the monument existed long before the Druids lived in Britain.

From writings by such Romans as the historian Tacitus and Julius Caesar, we know that Druids were the native priests, poets, and seers of Celtic Gaul (which later became France) and Britain when the Romans conquered northwestern Europe in the first century B.C. and the first century A.D. With great determination, Stukeley developed John Aubrey's idea about the Celts and priestly Druids of the late Iron Age as the possible builders of Stonehenge.

Stukeley knew that the Celts were among the first historically recorded people of pre-Roman Britain. But he romanticized and elaborated on Aubrey's hesitant suggestion that Stonehenge was created as a Druid temple. In fact, Stukeley completely indulged his passionate belief in this notion in his 1740 book *The History of the Religion and Temples of the Druids*. He embraced the idea and took it far beyond Aubrey's intent, not to mention the existing evidence.

His book captured the public fancy, and ever since, the Druids have been linked to Stonehenge in the popular imagination, even though archaeological evidence shows that the construction itself was at least 2,000 years old by the time the Druids came along.

The connection existed only in Stukeley's mind. For Stukeley, everything he observed about Stonehenge was somehow part of the Druid legend. He invented rites and sacrifices that no one had ever seen and for which there was no evidence. In the story he told so vividly, he painted Stonehenge as a Druid center. In spite of his fantasies, Stukeley was a very careful observer of archaeological sites and their landscapes who made wonderful drawings and records of the monuments.

Even today, in the 21st century, we still know little about the ancient Druids. Stukeley knew even less, but the doctor was hooked on his theory. In the late 1730s, Stukeley changed his life. He retired from his medical practice, married, and was ordained a clergyman in the Church of England. Then, dramatically, he transformed himself into the role of what he thought was an ancient Druid. He imagined incorrectly (from what little we know) that Druid ceremonies were very much like those of the Christians, even though the Druids were a pagan, non-Christian people.

In 1781, some 40 years after Stukeley published his book, a group enamored with his ideas founded the Ancient Order of the Druids. Today, the remnants of this order call themselves the Church of the Universal Bond. Its robed followers are the "Druids" who each summer since the early years of the 20th century have tried to celebrate the summer solstice at Stonehenge. There is no connection between the Druids and the prehistoric people who actually built and used the monument.

In this drawing from the 1720s, Stukeley depicted strange Druid rites at Stonehenge. Details include, on the right, buglers in a procession; on the left, Roman-looking soldiers with a flag; and various animal sacrifices.

2

The People Behind the Stones

This aerial view of Stonehenge in the snow highlights its place in the landscape. Clearly visible are the ditch and bank and the Avenue—beyond the modern road—which leads up to the Heel Stone.

If the Druids did not build Stonehenge, who did? We know from modern scientific dating methods that the prehistoric people who lived in southern Britain before 3000 B.C. began construction by building a small earth circle, called a henge, with a bank surrounded by a ditch. Different phases of the great stone monument were eventually built inside this circle between about 2500 and 1600 B.C. After 1500 B.C. there were no more standing stone monuments built at Stonehenge or elsewhere in Britain.

The first henges were built by British farmers at the end of the late Stone Age, the Neolithic. These farmers lived in small communities, with houses scattered among their fields. They made pottery and fashioned tools from flint and stone. They tended their crops and cared for their livestock. They traded goods across the countryside and participated in social activities, which included building earth and stone monuments.

The descendants of the Neolithic farmers, copper-using Beaker people, emerged around 2500 B.C. Archaeologists have named them the Beaker folk because of their distinctive pottery. They were among the first people to use metals such as copper and gold.

These people continued to develop and build circles and elaborate henges. Their sites included rings of stone or wood, often located near long avenues of stone and earth. Stonehenge is the remains of one of the more than 900 henges or earthworks still surviving today in Britain. Many more sites have been totally destroyed by farmers and urban development. Even so, some earthworks, which may have enclosed timber or stone circles, are located each year by aerial photography.

We may never have a definitive answer to the question, "Why did the builders go to all that trouble?" But with the evidence

These vessels were used by the Beaker folk for drinking. They were made of red or brown burnished ware and decorated with horizontal designs.

Avebury, some 20 miles north of Stonehenge, is an enormous circle of 98 Sarsen stones, 1,200 feet across, which encloses two smaller stone circles. It is surrounded by a high bank and ditch.

Scientific Dating

Because the builders of Stonehenge were prehistoric—that is, they did not have writing—they did not leave any records that tell us when the monument was built. Instead, archaeologists rely on various scientific methods to date the monument in its ancient landscape.

The carbon-14 (C-14) process, discovered in 1948, is one of the most important ways an archaeological site can be dated. The method is based on the fact that carbon is the essential building block of life and can be found in all living things. Organic materials such as antler, bone, and wood found at Stonehenge can be dated because C-14 decays in a slow and measurable way. The smaller the amount of C-14 found in the object, the older it is.

However, when experts compare C-14 dates to known dates from other sources, they realize that the C-14 dates are not accurate. For example, we know certain dates from the ancient Egyptian King lists. But when archaeologists use a C-14 date from a king's burial, it does not match up with the known date. The process has to be refined.

A new method has been devised using the world's oldest living trees, the 6,000-year-old Bristlecone pines. The tree's exact age has been determined by counting its rings. Then experts carbon-date the same tree sample and compare the two readings. Comparisons show how far off the C-14 dates are and set a standard for correcting or calibrating the C-14 date. Now uncorrected dates of about 2000 B.C. are recalibrated to about 2500 B.C., and dates of about 2500 B.C. are recalibrated to about 3200 B.C. The C-14 method can date objects up to 40,000 years and, with some special techniques, up to 70,000.

inferred from modern archaeology, Stonehenge was probably built for a combination of ritual, including seasonal festivals linked to the observation of the sun and possibly the moon. These ceremonies may have symbolized ideas about life, death, and the afterlife. Since it took some 1,200 to 1,500 years to build various phases of Stonehenge, there probably were different uses at different periods of time.

Perhaps if we look at the landscape around Stonehenge, we can better imagine what rituals were held there—although at the same time we must also take into account that the landscape changed over this long period of time. During the earliest days of the third millennium (from 3000 to 2000 B.C.), the forest was cleared and the first stones stood in the open, much as they do today.

The Stone Age ended around 2500–2000 B.C. as the Beaker people emerged in Britain with their cord-impressed pottery and metals. During this period, it must have been important to have a center for an entire range of religious rites relating to the community, to its ancestors as well as to its more recent dead. So, birth, marriage, life, and death ceremonies were probably part of these reassuring patterns of ritual.

Just over a mile west of Stonehenge are the Winterbourne Stoke Barrows. At the lower left is a Neolithic long barrow built 1,000 years before the round Bronze Age barrows above and to the right of it.

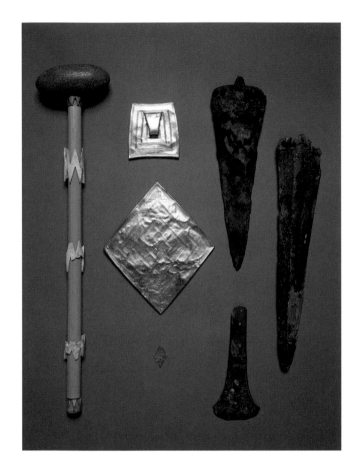

Bush Barrow, near Stonehenge, contained these symbols of power buried with an important man, probably a chief: on the far left is a mace with a stone head and bone decorations on the wooden staff; next to it, a gold breastplate and the small diamond-shaped gold piece that was attached to the man's robe. The barrow also contained two daggers; the hilt of the smaller dagger was decorated with thousands of gold pins.

The Beaker traditions were gradually replaced by Early Bronze Age customs from about 2000 B.C. Off in the distance, to the east and south of Stonehenge, there are small round burial mounds called barrows built during the Bronze Age. Archaeological evidence shows that the people in these graves were the elite of their group. They were often buried with gold and bronze objects of great beauty.

For example, inside a mound called Bush Barrow, located not far from Stonehenge and dating from 1800 B.C., a chief was laid on his back with a diamond-shaped sheet of gold on his chest and two daggers on his right. The hilt of one of these daggers was inlaid with several thousand tiny gold pins. The gold work was so distinctive that archaeologists believe that the same talented goldsmith might have crafted grave goods found in other barrows. In addition, a gold hook and another small diamond-shaped gold piece were attached to the chief's robe. Nearby were the remains of a mace, its shaft decorated with carved zigzag bronze mounts, its head of polished stone. A copper ax lay by the chief's right shoulder.

Since these people could bury their chiefs in this manner, they must have had a wealthy community. Also, judging from the number of these mounds still visible in the area, it must have been very important to these people to be buried near Stonehenge, and numerous bones of individuals have been found in the Aubrey Holes and the ditches of the monument itself.

As for solar observation, archaeologists' findings clearly indicate that the changing design of timber and stone was increasingly intended to highlight the summer solstice sunrise. The Heel Stone, placed about 75 feet from the bank and ditch, provided a sight line for the midsummer sunrise. Entrances changed through the years until finally a great earth-banked avenue was constructed. The avenue hooked up with a new entrance and lined up with the great stone trilithons—structures consisting of two upright stones with a cross-beam, or lintel, at the top—through which the rising sun shone on the summer solstice. Each year at dawn on the longest day of the year, June 21, a person standing at the center of Stonehenge could have looked through the stones to see the sun rise just left of the Heel Stone.

As seen from the Stonehenge circle, the midsummer sun rises between the Heel Stone and its now vanished twin.

In 1979 a rescue excavation in a narrow strip along the road near the Heel Stone uncovered new evidence: a huge hole that once might have held a twin to the Heel Stone. The stone had disintegrated and parts of it had been carried away, but evidence of the hole remained.

Before this discovery, experts wondered why the Heel Stone was placed so the midsummer sun rose just to its left rather than being in line with the rising sun. Actually, if the two stones sat side by side, as this evidence implies, together they would have framed the sunrise. Over the years, there has been a great deal of speculation that the stones were also aligned with the midwinter moon rising, eclipses, and even stars, but there is only sparse evidence to support these speculations.

3

Moving Tons of Stones

The smaller upright Blue-stone in the foreground contrasts with the fallen Sarsen lintel behind it. Despite their names, the stones are actually quite similar in color.

The stones at Stonehenge can be classified into two groups, Sarsens and Bluestones. Sarsen is the name given to a kind of sandstone formed on the seabed that covered this region of southern England some 70 million years ago. Large Sarsen boulders can be found in the Marlborough Downs, chalk hills located some 20 to 30 miles north of Stonehenge. It is a very hard stone, so it can be shaped only by chipping and hammering away at the surface.

The Sarsens of Stonehenge, the largest of which weighs 45 tons and is 30 feet in height (up to 8 feet of which is buried in the ground), were probably dragged using a great deal of human power from the Marlborough Downs. The mode of transport is still a matter of speculation, but the builders most likely used heavy wooden sleds. The huge stones would have had to be pulled through what is now the Vale of Pewsey, which has steep slopes in some places. The effort to move these huge, bulky stones not only would have been time-consuming, but also would have been a carefully directed and organized task. The workers would have been a team, cooperating under a leader who was in charge.

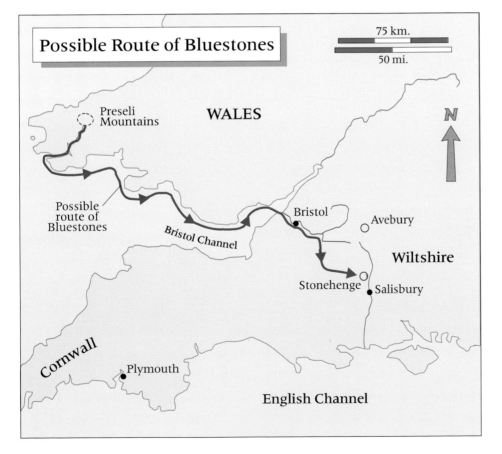

If the Bluestones were brought from the Preseli Mountains of Wales, it would have been difficult, if not impossible, to float the stones on rafts down the Bristol Channel, as some archaeologists have suggested. Dragging them on sleds over rough ground from the landing to the site would have been an even more demanding task.

Megaliths

Standing in lonely isolation, near Plouarzel, Brittany, in France this 36 foot high standing stone is one of dozens of menhirs in Brittany.

Stonehenge is only one of many megaliths built by Neolithic and Bronze Age people. Geographically megaliths range from Italy, Malta, Spain and western France, into northern Europe and throughout the British Isles. They have been dated from as early as 4500 B.C. to about 1500 B.C.

They vary in size and shape and fall into three broad categories. The simplest is the menhir, a single standing stone that may weigh hundreds of tons. A menhir can be as small as 2 feet or as high as 70 feet.

The second type occurs when menhirs are grouped together, in a circle or semicircle, or in rows called alignments. Stonehenge belongs in this category.

In the third category of megaliths are tombs—called dolmens, table stones, cairns, or cromlechs—which are capstones balanced on smaller slabs. When the tombs are covered with earth, they are called barrows. Some tomb megaliths are fully visible. There are many kinds of tombs including: single-chambered tombs; gallery graves, with as many as five chambers; and passage graves with a long corridor ending in a chamber. All use huge stones in their construction.

Pentre Ifan in southwest Wales is a tomb with its stone frame now exposed. Once covered with turf, its 108 foot length contains alignments of stones and ritual pits the purpose of which is unknown.

Bluestones, although they have only a vaguely bluish color, are very different from Sarsens. Volcanic rocks, only seven or eight feet in height, they are much smaller than the Sarsens and weighed an average of only 4 tons, while the Sarsens weighed an average of 26 tons. The Bluestones would have been easier to move. Since 1923 many archaeologists and geologists have proposed that the Bluestones used in Stonehenge came from the Preseli Mountains of southwest Wales, more than 130 miles away.

Gors Fawr, in Wales, is one of the 900 partially remaining circles still visible in Britain. It is the only stone circle in Wales made entirely of Bluestones, the same volcanic stones used at Stonehenge.

The Bluestones might have been quarried by pushing wooden wedges into natural cracks. Then, when the wedges were wetted, they expanded and split the rocks. The workers could have also produced cracks by lighting fires along breakage lines and then putting them out with water. The rapid cooling causes internal stress and cracks the rock, allowing it to be broken with stone hammers.

Because the Bluestones do not look very special, there might have been another reason to use these particular stones. Some archaeologists have proposed that they were part of an important ritual monument in Wales. Certainly, there are many standing stones and stone circles in that part of Britain; although only one of these, Gors Fawr, is constructed exclusively of Bluestones, the same type of stone found at Stonehenge. But possibly a legendary monument from a long-forgotten sacred place was dismantled, the stones brought from the Preselis, across the water, down the river, and overland to Salisbury Plain ready to be used at Stonehenge.

Not every expert agrees with this scenario. One prominent scholar, Aubrey Burl, wrote as recently as 1999 that "transportation by land and sea would have been so hazardous as to be

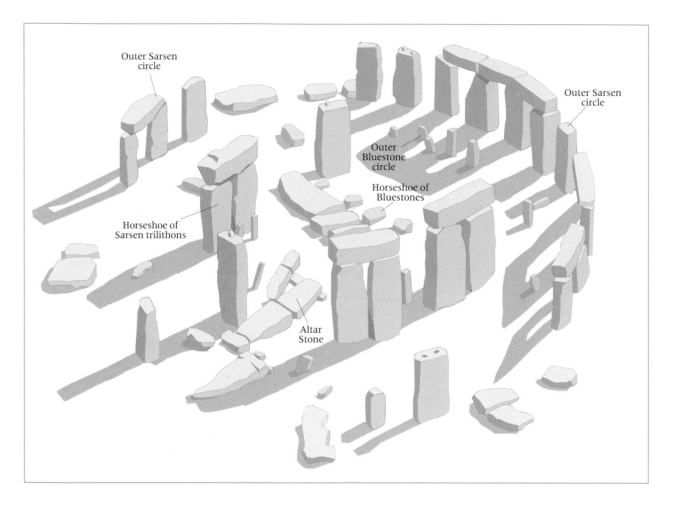

Outer Sarsen circle

Outer Sarsen circle

Outer Bluestone circle

Horseshoe of Bluestones

Horseshoe of Sarsen trilithons

Altar Stone

Remaining at Stonehenge today are 17 stones of what was once the Sarsen circle and 3 upright trilithons, that is, the Sarsens with lintels across the top. A few of the small Bluestones still stand but many have either fallen or lie broken on the ground.

improbable." He notes that one Bluestone had been deposited in a barrow near Stonehenge, centuries before the Bluestones were used in such great numbers at Stonehenge.

Burl has also suggested that the Bluestones were dragged from an area only 10 to 12 miles from Stonehenge. And, when no more local Bluestones could be found, the builders modified their more elaborate plans and settled for a "less impressive single circle of about 57 stones enclosing an elegant horseshoe of 19 pillars." We will never have a definitive answer, but Burl's alternative suggestion shows just how much speculation continues about the puzzling problems of building Stonehenge.

4

Years and Years of Building

In this drawing, the artist has imagined what Woodhenge might have looked like based on the wooden stumps that still remain. An alternative proposal is that the structure was an open-air circle with its posts connected by wooden lintels.

The earliest activity in the Stonehenge area dates from Mesolithic times, some 10,000 years ago. This was discovered in 1966 when archaeologists surveyed the area for clues before a new visitor center parking lot was constructed. The archaeologists found three large holes for posts located only 600 feet from the area that later became Stonehenge. They believed the posts supported a pinewood structure that could have been a house or even a cult site. Radiocarbon dates for the small pieces of pinewood left in the holes dated this feature to centuries before the beginnings of the stone circle's construction. Such a discovery suggests that the area already had a special significance even in those early times.

Phase 1
2950–2900 BC

Phase 2
2900–2400 BC

Phase 3
2550–1600 BC

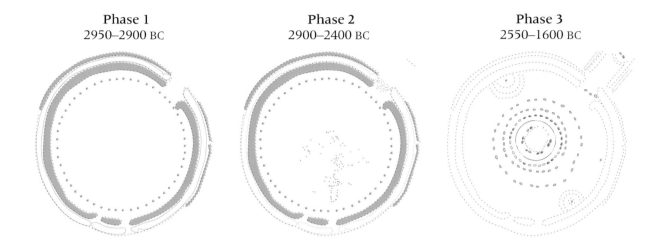

The three phases of Stonehenge progressed from Phase 1 (2950–2900 B.C.) with its bank and ditch and post holes, to Phase 2 (2900–2400) with its wooden buildings inside the circle. Phase 3 (2550–1600) was redesigned at least six times and was the most active period, during which the Sarsens and the Bluestones were erected.

Surveys by archaeologists of the landscape around Stonehenge show that the landscape changed rapidly from earlier times. Even before 3100 B.C. Neolithic farmers constructed causewayed enclosures by digging ditches that formed banks. Sections of the banks were broken by pathways, or causeways, leading into the enclosures, thus their name. This occurred not only at Stonehenge but in other parts of southern England as well.

Near Stonehenge were concentrations of long barrows that contained the remains of ancestors, accompanied by simple grave goods of pottery, flint, and bone. Often parallel banks and ditches, called cursus, were constructed nearby. The area was clearly a place of great significance even before the monumental stone circle was constructed.

The first construction at Stonehenge, between 2950 and 2900 B.C., was a henge, a ditch and circular bank 490 feet in diameter with a single entrance. Excavations have revealed that the henge was dug with picks made of deer antler and shovels made of the shoulder bones of cattle. After the Neolithic workers finished digging the ditch, they placed bones on either side of the entrance and at the bottom of the ditch. Around the inner edge of the ditch was the circle of 56 pits later known as the Aubrey Holes. Many of these holes contained flint, stone chips, and animal bones.

Aerial Discoveries

From as early as the 1920s up to the present day, pilots flying over England have discovered archaeological remains by their outlines. In 1923, O. G. S. Crawford, a well-known archaeologist, looking at negatives of photographs taken from the air, found a pair of thin parallel lines running cross-country between Stonehenge and Amesbury. He realized they were part of Stonehenge's Avenue.

In 1925 an experienced pilot who regularly flew over the countryside around Stonehenge noticed a circle with white chalk marks in a plowed field not far from the monument. As the season progressed and the wheat grew, the pilot realized he was seeing a wide, round ditch with a single causewayed entrance inside numerous closely-set rings of spots, which actually were traces of holes for wooden posts cut into the chalk. Squadron Leader Insall had discovered Woodhenge from the air.

Tourists at Woodhenge inspect the various size concrete posts marking the places where ancient pillars once stood.

An archaeologist carefully brushes the soil away from one of the antler tools found in the ditch at Stonehenge. These bone tools, which can be carbon dated, are one of the keys to dating the different building phases.

Shortly after the monument was given to the nation, the Society of Antiquaries of London sponsored Colonel William Hawley, an amateur archaeologist. He was given the job of making it safe for public visits and discovering new information. Between 1919 and 1926 Hawley made a series of major excavations and discoveries. He dug over half of the inner part of the site and excavated 32 out of the 56 Aubrey Holes as well as part of the perimeter bank and ditch. He found cremated human bones in several of the Aubrey Holes. Even though he was a careful worker, he did not have the background or resources to interpret the site as modern archaeologists would today. Yet from his findings, experts suspect that a timber structure known as a woodhenge was built in the center of the enclosure. The stone structure built later imitated this first wooden building.

Environmental evidence shows that the earliest Stonehenge was abandoned from about 2900 to 2550 B.C. It was covered by soil, which hid many of its original features. There were other sites nearby that must have drawn visitors. But the one called Durrington Walls, an enormous ditched structure with circular wood buildings, what we might call a superhenge, must have become the major attraction of its time.

From about 2550 to 2400 there was renewed activity at Stonehenge. Much of the henge ditch was filled in, and several cremated remains were buried there. Grooved ware and other decorated pottery styles, bone pins, and flint tools from this period have been found at the site. At its center, there was probably a large wooden building. Other wooden structures filled the northern entrance area and also south of the building, perhaps as gateways or barricades. Some think these buildings may have been part of an early astronomical observatory or a ceremonial structure.

The third phase of Stonehenge's construction, by far the longest, began about 2550 B.C. It was broken up into at least six sub-phases. Durrington Walls was gradually abandoned and people focused on Stonehenge instead. According to evidence uncovered by numerous archaeologists over the years, there were several stages of building, demolition, and rebuilding.

Experts estimate that the local chiefs and their communities redesigned or modified the monument at least six times over several hundred years, a period that included the end of the Neolithic era, the Beaker Period, and the Early Bronze Age. It was a time of great changes as metal began to be used and finely crafted objects of gold, bronze, amber, jet (a black, velvety stone), and bone were made, traded, and buried with the dead. The monumental complex we see today, the concentric stone circles, and the Avenue were constructed during this time.

First, the Bluestones were brought to the site and set up in pairs at the center. For some reason this arrangement was never finished and was dismantled. Soon afterwards the great Sarsen circle of 30 upright pillars began to be erected. Of these pillars, 17 still stand today. The stones stood some 22 feet high above ground and were topped by continuous capstones, called lintels, of carefully shaped Sarsens. At the center of the circle, a horseshoe-shaped arrangement of five pairs of trilithons (two stones with a lintel) opened toward the northeast and a new main entrance. This arrangement improved the sight lines from the rising sun through the site.

The Sarsens were tapered—narrower at the top than at the bottom. Shaping the Sarsens could not have been easy for the workers because of the hardness of the stone. The laborers pounded and chipped away at the rough stones with tools, probably hammerstones, so that they fitted the planners' designs.

When we look at the pillars from a distance, the tapering makes them look taller and more slender. Architects in more recent times, including the ancient Greeks, used the same device to give buildings added height and lightness. Just like their Neolithic ancestors, these builders used

Workers chipped stones off the Sarsens to make mallets of different sizes. With these stone tools, which range in size from a tennis ball to a soccer ball, workers shaped and dressed the huge Sarsen blocks. The hammerstones shown here were found at the site.

deer antler and oxen-bone shovels to excavate the ditches and the holes for the stones.

In order to make Stonehenge stable, strong, and secure, the builders used the mortise (socket or hole) and tenon (knob) system. They would gouge socket holes or sculpt knobs into the Sarsens. Then they would put stones together by fitting the knobs on top of the pillars into the sockets in the lintels. In this way, the immense stones were firmly attached.

In addition, the ends of the lintels were alternately tongued and grooved, so that the tongue on one end of the lintel fitted into the groove on the end of its neighbor. This method was also used when working with wood. Indeed, the mortise-and-tenon, tongue-and-groove technique was probably used at the nearby ancient site of Woodhenge. Experts agree that the similar construction methods used indicate that stone circles, including Stonehenge, are the descendants of the earlier wood-constructed sites.

So the stones were shaped, tapered, and their ends made ready for attaching to each other before they were put in the ground. The evidence to support this comes from the many stone chippings found in the holes and in the ditches.

The next challenge was putting the stones in their designated places. Through extensive experimental work and observation of the site, archaeologists know how the stones were placed and raised. For each stone, the workers would dig a huge hole with three straight sides and a fourth sloping one that was lined with wood. The wood lining may have been rubbed with animal fat in order to slide the immense stone in more easily. Then they

This drawing shows how a pit was dug with three straight sides and one angled. These stones were slid into place on rollers, and eventually rocks were put around the base to hold it firmly.

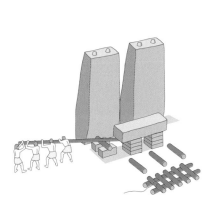  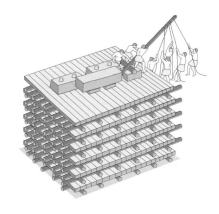

brought a Sarsen, one end of which had been chipped to a point, to the hole on a sled and slipped it point-first down the sloping side of the hole into place. To get the Sarsen upright, they probably constructed a tower of crossed logs to brace it and then used long poles to push it farther and farther into a vertical position.

To place the lintel on top of the upright Sarsens, they would have worked very slowly and with great care, because one slip could mean disaster and even death for some of the workers. Most experts believe that they rolled the lintel so it was parallel to where it would be placed on top of the two uprights. Then they would raise the stone off the ground, lifting it slowly while supporting it with wooden posts, perhaps only a few inches at a time. This log construction would grow higher and higher, eventually bringing the lintel level with the uprights, some 22 feet above the ground. Then the workers would carefully slide the lintel sideways so that it would fit precisely on the knob of the prepared Sarsen.

In the next phase, the abandoned Bluestones were placed into a single circle of about 57 stones enclosing a horseshoe of 19 pillars between the outer Sarsen circle and the inner Sarsen horseshoe. This final arrangement of Bluestones was added with the Altar Stone (which was made of sandstone) as the focal point, facing the entrance to the henge. For the next few centuries, the arrangements of the stones stayed about the same, and it was probably during this period that the henge was used most intensively.

This illustration of the laborious process of raising and placing the lintel shows how the workers used platforms and crossed timbers to support the lintel as it was levered up inches at a time.

The fallen Sarsen in the foreground probably stood upright as late as the 17th century. Drill holes on one side suggest that local people may have tried unsuccessfully to break up the stone and then found it too heavy and bulky to move when it could not be broken in pieces.

During this long third phase, various additions were made outside the main henge monument. The Heel Stone and the Slaughter Stone were added to mark the main line of sight of the rising midsummer sun. The Slaughter Stone was named because of its red stains, which, although they look something like bloodstains, were really caused by rainwater acting on the stone's iron content. In addition, inside the bank but outside the henge are four stones called the Station Stones, which formed a rectangle. Some think the Station Stones were markers for astronomical observations. However, accurate dating of these isolated stones is difficult.

The Avenue, built about 2100 B.C., was constructed of chalky earth banks set about 40 feet apart. It provided a grand ceremonial entrance to the great stone circle. The Avenue led people from the Avon River, more than a mile away, along a curving route. As it rounded sharply into the final straight approach, Stonehenge could be seen rising from the hillside. Experts have imagined processions of celebrants, dressed in their finery, walking toward the great monument. Their sudden view of Stonehenge was dramatic and stirring—just what the prehistoric builders must have intended.

A few final touches were added about 1600 B.C., when concentric rings of pits were dug outside the main Sarsen ring. Archaeologists call these pits the Y and Z holes. These holes were probably dug to hold stones or posts, but they were never placed and the scheme was abandoned. In fact, from this time onward, the whole site seems to fade gradually into disuse.

Archaeologists have tried to estimate the human effort in hours that was expended in these different phases. These communities had to cooperate in order to succeed at such a complex task. There must have been different generations of builders to envision the way Stonehenge should look over this long period, as well as planners to decide how the construction should be done, and numerous leaders or chiefs to organize large groups who would dig the ditches, quarry the stones, and transport and erect them. Possibly these were the important people buried in the rich, Bronze Age barrows around Stonehenge.

The third phase of Stonehenge, during which the Sarsen circle and trilithons were constructed, could have taken as many as 2 million hours of hard labor to complete. In comparison, the "causewayed camps," the great ditches that came before henges, may have required around 50,000 to 70,000 hours.

These estimates are very tentative. Another theory suggests that the workers could have hooked up teams of oxen to drag the sleds each carrying a heavy stone across the landscape. In 1997, wheeled cart tracks were found in another part of Britain dating to the Bronze Age, so it is possible that some of the stones were carried on wheeled carts. But even if the wheel had been available during the years when Stonehenge was erected, the great weight of the stones probably made sleds a more efficient choice.

These organized societies, often called Chiefdoms, managed to bring together enough people to move the huge stones over considerable distances, and to design and then master new technology to erect the architectural structure that is Stonehenge. The elite members of these communities were able to mobilize scattered groups of farmers and to inspire craftsmen to create the spectacular henge, as well as the artifacts associated with burials of their elite. For more than 16 centuries and for some 60 or 70 generations, Stonehenge was the focus of ritual, ceremony, and everyday life.

5

Abandoned but Not Forgotten

Over the years, artists have imagined what Stonehenge might have looked like at the height of its use. In this 19th-century depiction, there are snakes on the flags as well as Biblical images of the Ark of the Covenant and people dressed in European medieval costumes.

We have seen that thousands of years ago the people of Wessex created a site of special significance, one of the most impressive prehistoric monuments in Europe. They were also one of the richest British people of their time, as indicated by the clusters of barrows, that is, burial mounds, near Stonehenge that contained opulent grave goods. After 1500 B.C., there is no longer evidence of artifacts deposited at Stonehenge or use of the monument itself. It was left to disintegrate. What happened?

There is a worldwide phenomenon among other early long-established cultures of rapid and complete decline, which historians used to attribute to invasions by outsiders. More recently, however, experts think such falls were due to internal stresses. Sometimes farmers over-used their land so that population centers shifted to new regions.

Some experts suggest that one of the problems at Stonehenge was that it may have been a monument for elite groups of people. The inner circle, which is half the size of a modern tennis court, could have held only a small number of people at one time. The huge stones would have blocked the view of what was going on inside. And only a few people could have participated in the rites within the interior of the structure, even though great numbers of workers had participated in erecting the stones.

Another possible reason for the abandonment of Stonehenge after 1500 B.C. was the change in climate. There is evidence that Britain's climate became cooler beginning as early as 1800 B.C. Higher elevations were abandoned. Agriculture became more concentrated. People moved east to more productive areas. About 1400 B.C. the climate became cooler and wetter and remained so until 700 B.C. when it began to recover.

To make things worse, the early farmers had cleared much of the forest in the Neolithic and Early Bronze Age. This clearing removed the trees that had anchored the soil and regulated the water table. As a result, much of Britain was transformed from lush farmland and rich, pristine forest to heath, moors, bogs, and marsh.

Some experts suggest that the climate may have been affected by volcanic eruptions elsewhere in the world that are thought to have caused devastating dust clouds around 1159 B.C. These clouds might have lowered the temperatures because of the reduced sunlight and caused poor conditions for the plants to grow. If the people could not see the sunrise, the moon, or the stars so clearly, perhaps they felt there was no reason to congregate at a monumental construction dedicated to the sun and heavens.

All these events that made Britain cold, wet, cloudy, and more difficult to farm could have been the momentum that changed people's devotion to their religious beliefs and their society so that monuments were no longer important.

But the strongest argument for why Stonehenge went out of fashion is that Bronze Age society changed dramatically beginning about 1500 B.C. Changes included the fact that astronomy as observed from stone circles seems to have been abandoned. Instead, a "larger" world of trade and craftsmen seem to have participated in producing everyday tools and weapons for a different kind of society of villages and farms.

As social and economic trends shift, fashions change and people no longer honor the ancestors and monuments that had once been important to them. When people adopted new ideas and values, they stopped using, and even respecting, the old ceremonial centers, even a monument as conspicuous as Stonehenge.

By the Late Bronze Age, around 1000 B.C., farmers no longer respected the ancient stone monuments that once had been important to their ancestors. Farmers plowed close to the stone monuments and burial places, destroying the mounds and removing stones that lay in their way.

By 500 B.C. the so-called Celtic Iron Age of Britain was influenced by European population migrations, language and art, and earlier Bronze Age and Neolithic beliefs had been totally forgotten. So Stonehenge, as a prehistoric monument, may have simply

In 1899 people questioned the value of Stonehenge. This cartoonist jokes that Stonehenge might attract tourists with such amenities as the scale on the left, the restaurant with a waiter in the middle, and even a roller coaster in the background.

100   PUNCH, OR THE LONDON CHARIVARI.   [AUGUST 30, 1899.

HOW STONEHENGE MIGHT BE POPULARISED IF THE GOVERNMENT BOUGHT IT. SUGGESTION GRATIS.

become outdated. We will probably never have all the answers as to why the fashion changed.

People may have lost interest in Stonehenge in ancient times, but they rediscovered it many centuries later—as a tourist attraction as early as the 17th century. In Victorian times, at the turn of the 20th century, 20,000 or so visitors came calling each year. In 1951, when the Festival of Britain was held, 124,000 tourists visited Stonehenge. By 1971, there were 551,000 each year. Projections for the year 2000 were more than 1 million visitors each year. That would mean close to 3,000 visitors each day. Now, Stonehenge is being loved to death.

One of the greatest problems for Stonehenge in the 21st century is access. Gone are the days when people could wander freely among the Bluestones and the Sarsens. For more than 25 years, English Heritage, which manages the site, has directed visitors to a path circling the monument. In fact, after a series of disruptions by unruly revelers during the 1980s, a four-mile exclusion zone was established around the stone circle on the night of the summer solstice. Only in 1998 were organized groups allowed once again to schedule solstice visits. But in 1999, riot police had to be called after gatecrashers pushed down fences and climbed on the stones. In the year 2000, in honor of the new millennium, the area was opened to the public, but only for eight hours, from 11:30 P.M., June 20, to 7:30

In 1958 a 60-ton mobile crane was used to restore the stones that had fallen in 1797 and 1900. The stones were then encased in felt-padded steel cages and reset.

A.M., June 21. No camping, fires, dogs, or amplified music were allowed. English Heritage told the public, "It's not a party."

Recently, a Master Plan has been drafted for a new visitor center, less obtrusive parking, and walking access up to and among the stones. Also included is a plan for pathways from various points around the periphery of the monument.

Another pressing problem for the future of Stonehenge is the surrounding roads. Two heavily used highways run very close to the monument. Part of the new Master Plan is to build a medium length cut-and-cover tunnel that will make the traffic totally invisible from Stonehenge.

Stonehenge was an extremely special ceremonial place for more than 1,500 years. Can we learn more about it, protect it, and allow people full access to it at the same time? Answering this question will be a major challenge in the 21st century.

A recent visitor to Stonehenge listens to an audio tour for facts and figures about the monument as she walks around the site.

Interview with Caroline Malone

Nancy Stone Bernard How did you get interested in archaeology?

Caroline Malone I lived in a 700-year-old house in Battle, in Sussex, England, near the site of the A.D. 1066 Battle of Hastings, from the time I was five years old. In renovating the house, my family dismantled walls and in doing so, exposed layers of the house. There were layers and layers and always something beneath. That's where I got the idea of the layers of history!

NSB At what age did you decide to become an archaeologist?

CM When I was 14 or 15. Riding along the chalk downs covered with ancient burial mounds and hill forts, I realized I liked looking at ancient things in the landscape. They were very real to me.

NSB Did you have role models?

CM No, not real-person role models. But in the 1960s and 1970s, there was a marvelous TV program called the "Chronicle" series. They talked about figures such as Tutankhamun and I was inspired by the ancient cultures. Unfortunately, now TV research on archaeology is less thorough than it was in those years. It's often too quick and in too little depth.

Caroline Malone stands next to a chief's tomb from the first century B.C. in the gallery of Celtic Europe at the British Museum in London. The tomb was found in Hertfordshire in southeast England. (bottom) Nancy Stone Bernard sits on an outcrop of Bluestones during a visit to Wale's Preseli Mountains.

NSB Where have you done archaeological fieldwork?

CM I've worked in many places in England: in a Palaeolithic Neanderthal cave on the island of Jersey, which is one of the Channel Islands; I also worked at Neolithic, Bronze, and Iron Age sites. As a student I went to Italy and worked in Sicily. I've also excavated on the island of Malta.

NSB What were some of your most interesting digs?

CM I worked on the small island Gozo, part of the Mediterranean islands of Malta, for eight seasons at a cave site that dated from about 3000 B.C. The site related to the nearby remains of the Neolithic Ggantija temple. We excavated some 200,000 ancient "body parts" of buried humans from a population of at least 1,000 people. The cave had been part of a great megalithic complex and had been surrounded by a stone circle.

NSB Have you had funny experiences?

CM Rather than funny, the weird experience I had was in southern Italy in the province of Taranto. With a TV camera crew, we visited a cave called the Grotta Porta Badisco. It is one of a number of Neolithic painted caves that are found in that part of Italy. We struggled into the cave on our tummies and found that it was painted in red ochre and bat droppings with patterns and stick figures. The patterns on the walls were also found on pottery. It had a very strange feeling about it.

NSB Your most important or memorable discovery?

CM We dug up small funereal figurines on Malta in a huge cave that was 40 meters by 50 meters [about 120 by 150 feet]. Many were small female figures; another stone statuette was a double figurine with one figure holding a baby and one holding a cup. This little piece is about six inches wide and five inches high. Both figures had complicated hairdos.

NSB You've been curator at Avebury, editor of the British archaeology magazine *Antiquity*, and a professor at Cambridge University, in England, but recently you've accepted a job at the British Museum. What are your new duties?

CM I am head of the department of prehistory and early Europe, although I still have students at Cambridge and continue to edit the journal. I live in Cambridge with my archaeologist husband Simon Stoddart and two daughters, 12 and 8 years of age. When we are in the field, the girls enjoy digging with us, but I'm not sure if they will want to continue archaeology as a career. Right now, my biggest problem is a two-hour train commute to London and another two hours back to Cambridge each day.

NSB How have you been involved in work at Stonehenge?

CM When I was curator at Avebury, one of my roles was to provide a recommendation to World Heritage that included a Stonehenge/ Avebury description. They needed this information to be able to make a judgment on how the sites would be protected and included in UNESCO World Heritage plans. My report discussed both sites and their settings in their respective landscapes.

NSB Recently, there have been novels and movies of imagined ceremonies: the people, the villains, and the heroes who built Stonehenge. What are your impressions of Stonehenge's builders, their everyday life, and their ceremonies?

CM There is new evidence that Stonehenge and the Wessex Bronze Age people who lived there were an increasingly unsettled society. There is more evidence of crowding; so there was competition and rivalry and possibly power struggles, perhaps using a sense of mystery to control people. There is no way we can know about the individuals, heroes or villains. Collective communal monuments such as Stonehenge were a product of a stratified society where there was probably great control. There were also bursts of organization. Others have seen a steady progression but to me the bursts probably make more sense. Stress may have pushed the times of increased building.

NSB There is now a Master Plan for making Stonehenge more accessible to the public. What is your impression of the Master Plan?

CM It's probably too optimistic. Stonehenge needs a radical, sensitive presentation. There shouldn't be commercialism; it must be presented absolutely right. Irreparable damage could be done, for example, by redoing the car park [parking lot]. Building and funding the tunnel is a major problem, but most important, the tunnel shouldn't erupt near the barrow cemeteries to the west. New roads could cause more damage to the landscape.

It's almost better to do nothing than to dig helter-skelter. What's so precious about Stonehenge is that there is a delicate landscape around it. The projected figure of 120 million pounds for the building of the tunnel is off-putting when English Heritage budgets perhaps only 100 million pounds for all of England each year. There is no part of the planning that can be divorced from this world-class site. In the long run it will happen, but it is a matter of government will.

NSB What's your advice to a young person who wants to make archaeology a career?

CM Stick with it! Get experience, a whole range of experience and skills. You can't be a professor straight out of university. Learn to be an enthusiastic communicator. Archaeology talks through the people who do it, not directly. Write, talk, draw, communicate the past to the present. Enjoy it. It's fun to do and has an important social role in modern society!

Glossary

Aubrey Holes An early feature of Stonehenge, these 56 holes are located inside the bank and ditch. Rediscovered in the 20th century and named after John Aubrey, the gentleman scholar who first noted them in 1666.

barrow A human-made mound of earth built to cover single or multiple burials.

Beaker folk Groups of people from Europe who first emerged in Britain around 2500 B.C., named for their distinctive decorated pots, called beakers.

Bluestones Stones with a slight bluish cast, composed mainly of a volcanic rock, dolerite, weighing about four tons on average.

Bronze Age Followed the Neolithic era and began about 2500 B.C. and ended in 1200 B.C.. During this period people began to use copper and then bronze, a mixture of copper and tin.

causewayed enclosure A roughly circular earthwork made of banks and ditch segments with one or more entrances. They were the predecessors of such sites as Stonehenge and Avebury.

cursus A pair of parallel banks and ditches that runs for a considerable distance across the countryside and can often be aligned on long barrows.

Druids Priests, poets, and seers of the Celtic people, who probably arrived in Britain from Europe in the first millennium B.C. The Druids did not build Stonehenge.

grooved ware pottery Made by later Neolithic people about 2600–2400 B.C., these vessels are distinguished by wide grooved decoration.

Heel Stone An unshaped Sarsen stone standing about 75 feet to the northeast of Stonehenge that, with a similar stone that used to stand beside it, framed the rising midsummer sun, as seen from the center of Stonehenge.

henge A roughly circular earthwork first built in the late Neolithic and Early Bronze Age (between 2700 and 2200 B.C.) consisting of a ditch and bank of earth with one to four entrances.

lintel A stone or timber beam placed across the top of two uprights.

megaliths Large stone structures built in Neolithic and Bronze Age times. Found worldwide, these constructions are considered the earliest architecture in the world.

mortise-and-tenon system A method of construction that involves fitting large knobs, called tenons, into holes or sockets, called mortises. At Stonehenge, the lintels were slowly lifted up so that their holes fit into the knobs on top of the Sarsens.

Neolithic era Spanned from about 4000 to 2500 B.C. in Britain.

prehistory The period before history was written.

Sarsen The largest stones at Stonehenge. Formed of limestone, some are as tall as 22 feet above ground (plus 8 feet buried in the ground), and some weigh up to 45 tons.

solstice In the Northern Hemisphere, either the longest day of the year (June 21), also called midsummer; or, in winter, the shortest day of the year (December 21).

trilithon Two upright stones with a cross-beam (lintel) stone placed across the top.

Wessex The area of central southern Britain that includes the counties Wiltshire, Dorset, Berkshire, Somerset, and Hampshire.

Further Reading

Burl, Aubrey. *Great Stone Circles: Fables, Fictions, Facts.* New Haven, Conn.: Yale University Press, 1999.

———. *Prehistoric Stone Circles.* Aylesburg, U.K.: Shire Archaeology: 1983.

———. *The Stone Circles of the British Isles.* New Haven, Conn.: Yale University Press, 1979.

Chippindale, Christopher. *Stonehenge Complete.* 1983. Rev., New York: Thames and Hudson, 1994.

Gibson, Alex. *Stonehenge and Timber Circles.* Stroud, U.K.: Tempus, 2000.

Malone, Caroline. *Avebury.* London: Batsford/English Heritage, 1989.

———. *Neolithic Britain.* Stroud, U.K.: Tempus, 2001.

Manley, John. *Atlas of Prehistoric Britain.* New York: Oxford University Press, 1989.

Mass, Wendy. *Stonehenge.* San Diego: Lucent, 1998.

Mohen, Jean-Pierre. *The World of Megaliths.* New York: Facts on File, 1990.

Pitts, Mike. *Hengeworld.* London: Arrow, 2001.

Scarre, Chris. *Exploring Prehistoric Europe.* New York: Oxford University Press, 1998.

Souden, David. *Stonehenge: Revealed.* New York: Facts on File, 1997.

Wernick, Robert, and the editors of Time-Life Books. *The Monument Builders.* New York: Time-Life, 1973.

Stonehenge and Related Sites in Southwest England

STONEHENGE, WILTSHIRE

A UNESCO World Heritage site located two miles west of Amesbury at the junction of the A303 and A344/360. It is nine miles from the nearest train station at Salisbury, and is open year round. The entry fee includes an audio tour. More information about visiting Stonehenge can be found at 011-44-1980-624715 or at the English Heritage website, www.english-heritage.org.uk.

AVEBURY, WILTSHIRE

Located on the B4003 just off the A4.

An immense and impressive henge covering 28 acres. Nearby antiquities include Windmill Hill, the Avenue and Sanctuary, Silbury Hill, and West Kennet Long Barrow. Just outside Avebury's bank and ditch is the Alexander Keiller Museum, which contains finds from the sites. There is free access to the stones at any reasonable time.

BOSCAWEN-UN CIRCLE, CORNWALL

Located on the southwest peninsula of Britain, 1,500 feet from the A30 Penzance–Land's End highway.

A circle of 19 granite stones with a pointed quartz pillar in the center. This is one of many stone circles in the vicinity, but all have been weathered by 50 centuries of winters. Some have fallen, some have been replaced incorrectly, and others have simply disappeared. Visitors have free access.

STANTON DREW, SOMERSET

Located far from large towns, some 30 miles west of Avebury, 6 miles south of Bristol, which has the nearest train station, and just east of Stanton Drew Village.

Composed of three stone circles of the Early Bronze Age, of which the Great Circle is the second largest stone circle in Western Europe after the outer ring at Avebury. Two of the circles had "avenues" of standing stones leading to them. In 1997, a magnetometer study showed that this is a much more elaborate and important site than archaeologists had ever thought. Visitors approach the main group of stones through Court Farm for a small fee.

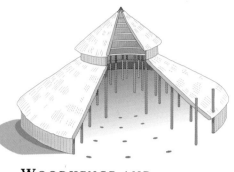

WOODHENGE AND DURRINGTON WALLS, WILTSHIRE

Located about 12 miles southeast of Stonehenge, just to the west of the A345.

Woodhenge was a wooden version of Stonehenge built and used around 2800–2500 B.C. Now, concrete cylinders, varying in width to show the different sizes of the disintegrated wooden posts, mark the places where the posts that supported the structure once stood. Its neighbor, the huge Durrington Walls, can best be seen by looking north from the entrance to Woodhenge. This monument dwarfs its contemporaries Woodhenge and Stonehenge with banks that are ⅓ of a mile in diameter and a ditch some 18 feet deep. Badly damaged over the centuries, there is little left for visitors to see today, only the outlines of the bank and ditch. Visitors have free access to both sites.

Index

Picture Credits

Ashmolean Museum: 17; Private Collection of Nancy Stone Bernard: 22, 23, 27, 39: Bodleian Library, University of Oxford, MS. Top. gen. c. 24, fol. 64v and Ms Top Gen b 53 f29-30r: 11, 13; Private Collection/The Stapleton Collection/Bridgeman Art Library: 34; British Library: 9, 10; Courtesy of Margaret Dermott: 38; English Heritage Photographic Library: cover, 1, 14, 15, 19, 32; Photri-Microstock: 20; Punch Magazine: 36; ©Brian Seed: cover inset, 28, 37; Gary Tong: 6, 8, 21, 24, 26, (25, 30, 31—adapted from illustrations in David Souden's *Stonehenge: Mysteries of the Stones and Landscape,* 1997); Wiltshire Heritage Museum: frontispiece, 4, 5, 15, 18.

Caroline Malone studied prehistoric archaeology at Cambridge University, and researched the Neolithic and Bronze Age of Italy and Malta before becoming the curator of the Alexander Keiller Museum at Avebury. She then worked as an inspector of ancient monuments in England, before teaching for ten years at Bristol and Cambridge Universities. She is now the keeper of the department of prehistory and early Europe at the British Museum.

Nancy Stone Bernard has written several books on archaeology for young people. She founded and is the director of the Archaeological Associates of Greenwich, Connecticut, a non-profit organization dedicated to educating the general public about archaeology. She served for six years on the governing board of the Archaeological Institute of America as its education chair. She has taught continuing education classes in archaeology and an enrichment program in prehistory to pre-collegiate students, first in Los Angeles, California, and for many years in Greenwich, Connecticut. She is currently on the editorial advisory board of *DIG* magazine.

Brian Fagan is Professor of Anthropology at the University of California, Santa Barbara. He is internationally known for his books on archaeology, among them *The Adventure of Archaeology*, *The Rape of the Nile*, and the *Oxford Companion to Archaeology*.

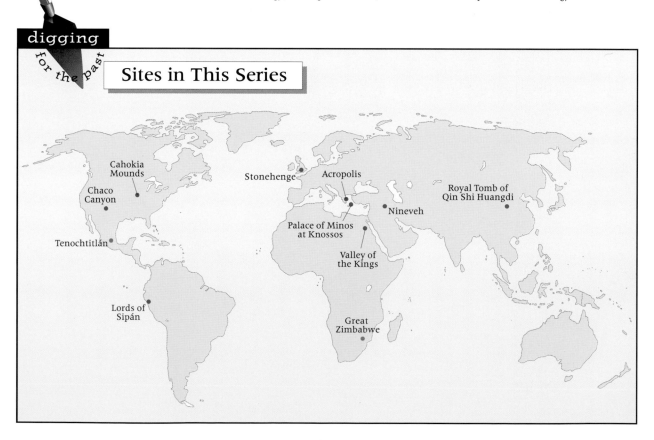

digging
for the past

Sites in This Series